WORLD OF WOW WONDER

I didn't know that

Get ready to hear your kids say, "Wow! I didn't know that!" as they dive into this fun, informative, question-answering series of books! Students—and teachers and parents—will learn things about the world around them that they never knew before!

This approach to education seeks to promote an interest in learning by answering questions kids have always wondered about. When books answer questions that kids already want to know the answers to, kids love to read those books, fostering a love for reading and learning, the true keys to lifelong education.

Colorful graphics are labeled and explained to connect with visual learners, while in-depth explanations of each subject will connect with those who prefer reading or listening as their learning style.

This educational series makes learning fun through many levels of interaction. The entertaining information combined with fantastic illustrations promote learning and retention, while question and answer boxes reinforce the subject matter to promote higher order thinking.

Teachers and parents love this series because it engages young people, sparking an interest and desire in learning. It doesn't feel like work to learn about a new subject with books this interactive and interesting.

This set of books will be an addition to your home or classroom library that everyone will enjoy. And, before you know it, you too will be saying, "Wow! I didn't know that!"

"People cannot learn by having information pressed into their brains. Knowledge has to be sucked into the brain, not pushed in. First, one must create a state of mind that craves knowledge, interest, and wonder. You can teach only by creating an urge to know." - Victor Weisskopf

© 2014 Flowerpot Press

Contents under license from Aladdin Books Ltd.

Flowerpot Press
142 2nd Avenue North
Franklin, TN 37064

Flowerpot Press is a Division of Kamalu LLC, Franklin, TN, U.S.A. and
Flowerpot Children's Press, Inc., Oakville, ON, Canada.

ISBN 978-1-4867-0339-5

Concept, editorial, and design by
David West Children's Books

Illustrators:
Ross Watton, Jo Moore

American Edition Editor:
Johannah Gilman Paiva

American Redesign:
Jonas Fearon Bell

Copy Editor:
Kimberly Horg

Educational Consultant:
Jim Heacock

Printed in China.

I didn't know that some planes hover

I didn't know that

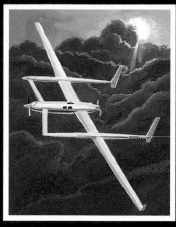

Introduction

Did you know that one plane had 200 wings? That some planes have none? That helicopters can fly upside down when they loop-the-loop?

Discover for yourself amazing facts about flying machines, from the earliest hot air balloons to the latest computer-controlled machines that can change shape as they fly.

 Watch for this symbol, which means there is a fun project for you to try.

 **True or false?** Watch for this symbol and try to answer the question before reading on for the answer.

Don't forget to check the borders for extra amazing facts!

I didn't know that

you can fly on hot air. As air heats up, it expands and becomes lighter than the air around it. If you fill a balloon with hot air, it will rise up. Gas burners heated the air in this balloon (right).

The Montgolfier brothers made this famous balloon (left) from linen and paper. It carried two men across Paris on the first-ever manned flight in November 1783. The air was heated by burning straw.

Balloon pilots rely on the wind for speed and direction. In 1987, Richard Branson and Per Lindstrand flew all the way across the Atlantic in a balloon—although Don Cameron and Christopher Davey set the long distance record of 2,074 miles (3,338 km) in 1978.

Can you find the dinosaur-shaped balloon?

! The first hydrogen-filled balloon also flew in 1783.

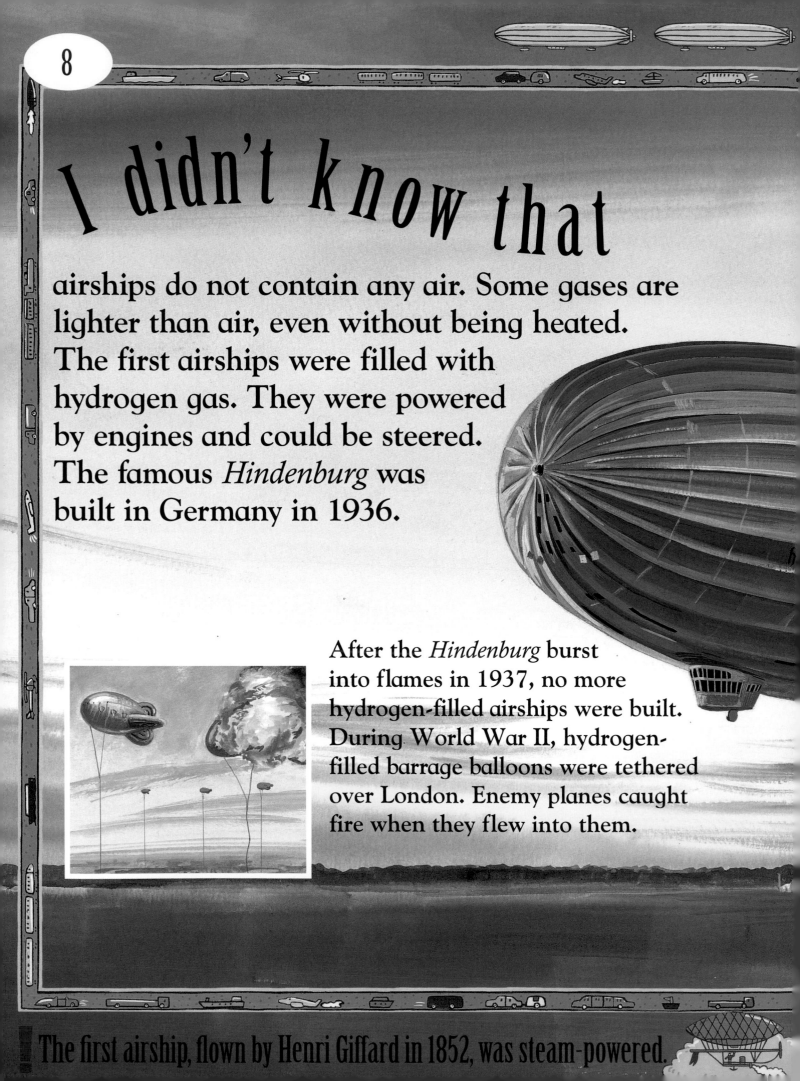

I didn't know that

airships do not contain any air. Some gases are lighter than air, even without being heated. The first airships were filled with hydrogen gas. They were powered by engines and could be steered. The famous *Hindenburg* was built in Germany in 1936.

After the *Hindenburg* burst into flames in 1937, no more hydrogen-filled airships were built. During World War II, hydrogen-filled barrage balloons were tethered over London. Enemy planes caught fire when they flew into them.

The first airship, flown by Henri Giffard in 1852, was steam-powered.

Modern airships are filled with helium gas. Helium gas is lighter than air, but it won't catch fire. This airship (right) can carry 20 passengers. It uses swiveling propellers when taking off and landing.

Hindenburg

Compare a helium-filled balloon with an ordinary one filled with air. Which one floats up on its own? Make sure you don't let go!

I didn't know that

some planes fly without engines. Once a glider has been towed into the air, it uses rising currents of hot air (thermals) to gain height. The curved shape of the wings keeps the glider airborne as it moves forwards.

Can you find the gliding gull?

The German aviator Otto Lilienthal (left) made over 2,000 glides before crashing to his death in 1896. His gliders were very similar to modern hang gliders.

Hang glider

True or false?
The Space Shuttle is a glider.

Answer: True
When the Space Shuttle reentered the Earth's atmosphere on its way home, it would glide halfway around the world before it came in to land.

Glider

Many of the first "heavier than air" flying machines that were tested in the early 1900s were gliders. The Wright brothers experimented with gliders for four years before their first powered flight in 1903.

! In 1849, a triplane glider lifted a 10-year-old boy into the air.

I didn't know that

some planes had three wings. Biplanes and triplanes were strengthened by the struts joining the wings. Triplanes got more lift from the shorter wings and made useful fighter planes.

The *Phillips Multiplane* of 1907 had 200 narrow, slat-like wings. Its designer, Horatio Phillips, gave it up after a few disappointing tests.

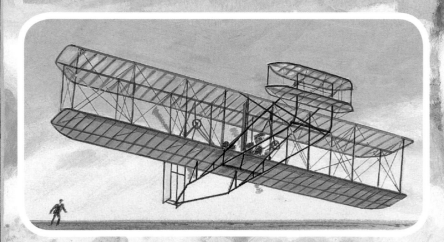

The Wright brothers' first powered flight in 1903 was in a biplane. They had spent many months making an engine that would be light enough.

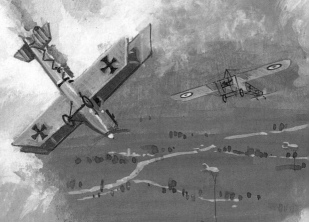

Can you find the *Bleriot monoplane?*

Fokker DRI

Alcock and Brown's *Vickers Vimy Bomber*

True or false?
A biplane was the first plane to cross the Atlantic.

Answer: True
It was a *Vickers Vimy Bomber* flown by British pilots Sir John William Alcock and Sir Arthur Whitten Brown in 1919.

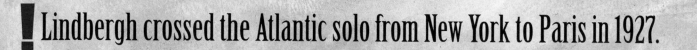

! Lindbergh crossed the Atlantic solo from New York to Paris in 1927.

I didn't know that

planes can land on water. Some early planes used the sea as a runway. A seaplane crossed the Atlantic in 1919, stopping to refuel. Passengers could fly long distances in the 1930s in flying boats like this *Boeing 314*.

The German *Junkers F13* that appeared in 1919 could be fitted with floats, wheels, or even skis. It was used to open up routes in remote areas of Russia and China.

The first airmail services started in Australia in 1914 and the USA in 1918. Flying boats were used to increase the service in the 1930s.

Boeing 314

The wooden *Spruce Goose* was the largest seaplane ever. It only flew once.

The latest flying boat is the *Sea Wing* (right), made in Tasmania. It is actually a boat, but it takes off from the water and flies above the water at a speed of 160 knots. It can fly in even rougher weather than a helicopter.

AMERICAN AIRWAYS SYSTEM

NC 18604

True or false?
The first seaplane flew in 1910.

Answer: True
Henri Fabre took off from a lake in the seaplane *Canard*. He flew for one-and-a-quarter miles (2 kilometers), just 13 feet (4 meters) above the water.

I didn't know that

a *Comet* was the first jet airliner. In 1952, passengers were thrilled by their fast, comfortable flight from London to Johannesburg in the new British-designed jet. Two years later, two *Comets* broke up in mid-air and the plane had to be redesigned.

Can you find the pilot?

Comet

The first battle between high-speed, jet-powered aircraft took place in 1944 when a British *Gloster Meteor* intercepted a pilotless *Doodlebug* (German flying bomb) over London.

The smallest jet plane, the *Silver Bullet*, weighs about as much as three people.

True or false?

You can't travel faster than the speed of sound.

Answer: False
Concorde (above right) first flew faster than the speed of sound (Mach 1) in 1969. You can sometimes hear the sonic boom made by a supersonic aircraft.

Future flight may be faster in space where there is no air friction. Planes would need ramjets to hop above the atmosphere.

I didn't know that

some planes are rocket-powered. Liquid-fueled rocket engines power the fastest planes. The *X-15s* were experimental aircraft. In 1967, the *X-15 A-2* reached 4,426 mph (7,123 km/h)—Mach 5.81.

X-15 Rocket plane

Can you find the bomber that launched *X-15*?

Chuck Yeager was the first pilot ever to go supersonic. He flew in a *Bell X-1* at 668 mph (1,075 km/h)— Mach 0.88.

 **True or false?**
Planes have to have wings to fly.

X-24A

Answer: False
This *X-24A* was used for NASA research into a plane that got its lift from the shape of the whole body and not just the wing. In 1970, it flew at 783 mph (1,260 km/h)—Mach 1.03.

Some very speedy cars use rocket power, too. In 1970, the *Blue Flame* (below) managed a record speed of 627 mph (1,009 km/h.) This is still the record for a rocket car.

Burning rocket fuel produces hot gases, which expand and escape downwards, thrusting the rocket upwards. See how this works by blowing up a balloon and watching it shoot forward as the air escapes.

I didn't know that

planes can change shape. Modern fighter planes change shape in mid-air. The *Panavia Tornado* takes off with its wings extended, but when it flies at top speed, they are swept right back.

True or false?
Planes can be invisible.

Answer: True
The unusual-looking *Lockheed F-117 Stealth Bombers* are designed to absorb or deflect radar signals, which means that they don't show up on radar screens.

Lockheed F-117 Stealth Bomber

! *The Flying Wing, built in 1950, was just that—shaped like an enormous wing.*

Panavia Tornado with wings swept back.

Some new military aircraft look backwards! The wings on this NASA *X-29* (above) face forward and the tailplanes are in front of the main wings.

Panavia Tornado with wings extended outwards.

The fastest jet-powered aircraft is the *Lockheed SR-71* (right), a spy plane known as *Blackbird*. It flies at speeds higher than 1,975 mph (3,178.5 km/h)—Mach 2.59.

I didn't know that

helicopters can fly upside down—when they loop-the-loop! And, unlike other aircraft, they can fly backwards and sideways too. The rotor blades have an aerofoil shape that creates lift as they rotate.

Apache AH-64

Helicopters can move vertically and hover, so they're very useful for rescuing people from a tight spot—such as a busy motorway, a mountain peak, or a stormy sea.

The autogiro can't hover like a helicopter. Its main rotor has no engine to power it. The engine only powers the propeller. This drives it forward. The rotor then rotates in the wind and produces lift.

Look for natural helicopters! Some tree seeds are dispersed with "rotors." Watch sycamore or ash "keys" as they spin away from the tree on the wind.

23

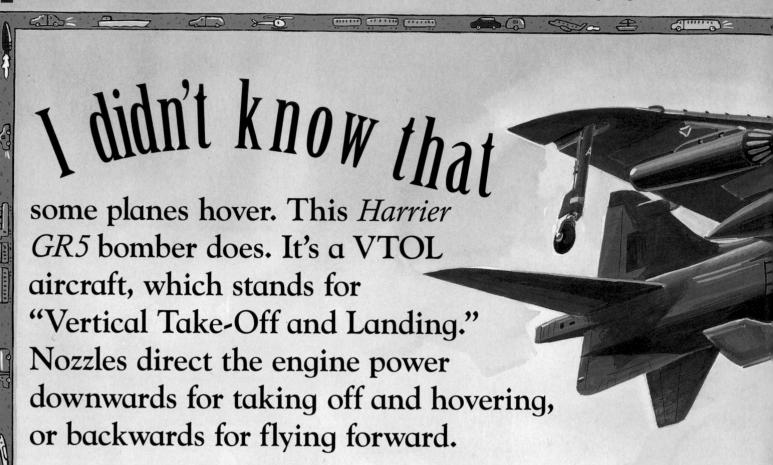

I didn't know that

some planes hover. This *Harrier GR5* bomber does. It's a VTOL aircraft, which stands for "Vertical Take-Off and Landing." Nozzles direct the engine power downwards for taking off and hovering, or backwards for flying forward.

This *Osprey* is a strange bird— a cross between a plane and a helicopter! The rotors are upright for vertical take-off and then tilt forwards for normal flight.

Planes that can take off and land at a steep angle are useful in built-up city areas. This little *DASH-7* is landing at London City Airport. It is a Short Take-Off and Landing (STOL) plane.

Harrier Jump-jet

Now humans can hover with a flying belt! A jet of superheated air rushes downwards from a jet-pack, thrusting the person up off the ground—but only for 28 seconds!

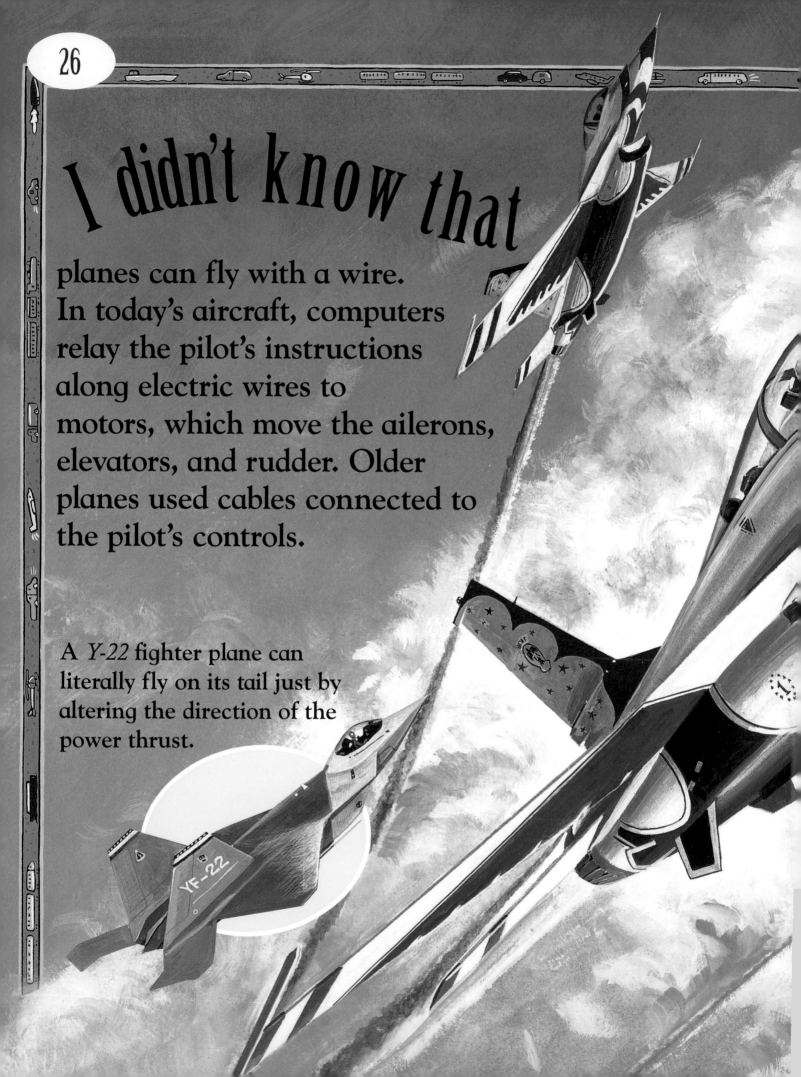

I didn't know that

planes can fly with a wire. In today's aircraft, computers relay the pilot's instructions along electric wires to motors, which move the ailerons, elevators, and rudder. Older planes used cables connected to the pilot's controls.

A *Y-22* fighter plane can literally fly on its tail just by altering the direction of the power thrust.

Skilled pilots can perform
some amazing stunts.
Although it looks
scary when they
stall (stop) and then
restart the engines,
the pilots know what
they are doing!

stall

steep dive with engine cut

engine restarted

steep climb

loop-the-loop

pull out of
dive

barrel roll

F-16 Fighting Falcon
American display team

True or false?
People walk
on wings.

Answer: True
In the 1920s and 30s, "wing walkers" were strapped to the wing
of a low-flying plane to advertise a product or a film.

I didn't know that

planes could be pedal-powered. The *Gossamer Albatross* was pedaled across the English Channel in 1979. It only weighed as much as a small child! The pedals turned the propeller.

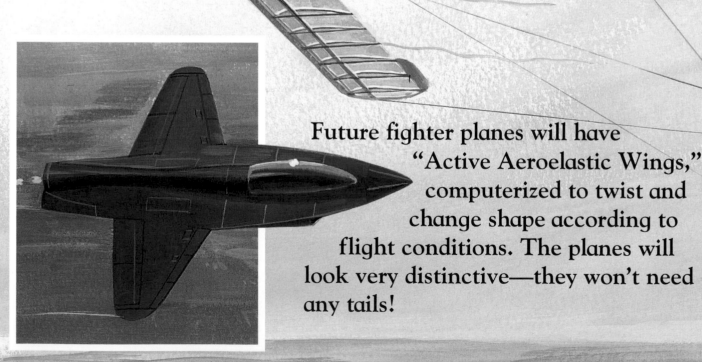

Future fighter planes will have "Active Aeroelastic Wings," computerized to twist and change shape according to flight conditions. The planes will look very distinctive—they won't need any tails!

Back in 1485, Leonardo da Vinci sketched designs for man-powered flight.

Voyager is an unusual light aircraft that flew non-stop around the world on a single tank of fuel.
The two pilots spent the nine-day journey in a pod that was only about two feet (60 cm) wide. Ouch!

In the Greek tale, Daedalus and Icarus flew out of captivity using wings of feathers and wax. But Icarus flew too close to the sun—and his wings melted!

Gossamer Albatross

Gossamer Albatross

DUPONT

MERCURY

Glossary

Aerofoil
Shape best suited to flight. The curved upper surface breaks up the airflow so that air pressure above is lower than air pressure below.

Ailerons, elevators, and rudder
Movable panels on wings, tailplane, and tail for tilting and turning plane.

Airship
Boat-shaped, gas-filled balloon that is power-driven and steerable.

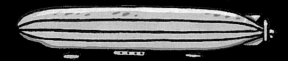

Atmosphere
Air surrounding the Earth.

Biplane
Plane with two sets of wings, one above the other.

Glider
Aircraft, without engines, that relies on air currents to stay in the air.

Jet
In a jet engine, air is sucked in, heated so it expands, and forced out in a jet that moves the aircraft forwards.

Lift
The force that keeps an airplane up, created when the air pressure below is higher than the air pressure above.

Mach 1
The speed of sound, named after physicist Ernst Mach. Mach 2 is twice the speed of sound.

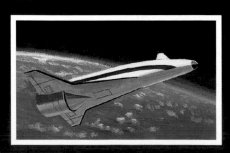

Mercury

A seaplane that was lifted into the air by a bigger aircraft to save fuel. It then set a straight-line distance record of 5,962 miles (9,595 km).

Propellers

Blades that rotate in air or water to move a plane or a boat along.

Radar

Stands for RAdio Detection And Ranging, used for detecting objects by bouncing radio waves off them.

Ramjet

A kind of jet engine that can provide extra power only when the aircraft is moving.

Rotor

Rotating blade that breaks up airflow to give lift.

Supersonic

Faster than the speed of sound. A supersonic aircraft breaking the sound barrier makes a "sonic boom" as shock waves reach the Earth.

Tailplane

A small, horizontal wing usually at the tail end of an aircraft.

Thrust

The force that pushes an aircraft forward.

Index

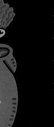